PIONEERS OF SCIENCE

ISAAC NEWTON

Douglas McTavish

The Bookwright Press
New York • 1990

Pioneers of Science

Leonardo da Vinci
Isaac Newton

First published in the
United States in 1990 by
The Bookwright Press
387 Park Avenue South
New York, NY 10016

First published in 1990 by
Wayland (Publishers) Limited
61 Western Road, Hove
East Sussex, BN3 1JD, England

Library of Congress Cataloging-in-Publication Data
McTavish, Douglas.
     Isaac Newton / by Douglas McTavish.
        p. cm. — (Pioneers of science)
     Includes bibliographical references.
     Summary: Describes the scientific and mathematical discoveries of
Isaac Newton through a biographical approach to his work, which
resulted in modern science.
     ISBN 0–531–18351–3
     1. Newton, Isaac, Sir, 1642–1727—Juvenile literature.
2. Physics—History—Juvenile literature. 3. Astronomy—History—
Juvenile literature. 4. Physicists—Great Britain—Biography—
Juvenile literature. [1. Newton, Isaac, Sir, 1642–1727. 2. Scientists.]
I. Title. II. Series.
QC16.N7M375 1990
530'.092—dc20
[B]   90–31936
[92]   CIP
                                                           AC

Typeset by Rachel Gibbs, Wayland
Printed in Italy by Rotolito Lombarda S.p.A.

Contents

1 ▼ Early Life

Isaac Newton was born on Christmas Day, 1642, in the small village of Woolsthorpe in Lincolnshire, England. His father, Robert, was a local farmer. Robert never knew his son because he died three months before the boy was born. Isaac was born prematurely and was so weak that he was not expected to live for more than a few hours.

Newton was born at Woolsthorpe Manor, near Grantham in Lincolnshire, England.

The Grammar School at Grantham, where Isaac studied.

When Isaac was three years old his mother, Hannah, married again. Her new husband was a wealthy clergyman, the Reverend Barnabas Smith. Hannah moved to live with him in the neighboring village of North Witham, leaving Isaac at Woolsthorpe. For the next ten years Isaac was brought up by his grandmother. He was sent first to the local day school and then, when he was twelve, to the King's School in Grantham, about six miles away. We know little about his time at school, except that he was not at first a very good scholar. However, he soon developed into the school's best student. He seems to have been a rather lonely child who kept very much to himself and did not easily make friends with his classmates.

In 1656 Isaac's mother became a widow again when the Reverend Smith died. She moved back to Woolsthorpe and took Isaac out of school to run the farm. He did not make a good farmer; he spent too much of his time thinking about mathematics and forgot his duties. After a time, Isaac's uncle, William Ayscough, persuaded Hannah to send her son back to

In 1661 Isaac began his studies at Trinity College, Cambridge. This picture shows the Great Court and Chapel at the College.

school to prepare himself to go to college. He told her that Isaac had an "extraordinary talent" and that it would be a great loss to the world if he did not use it. And so, in 1660, Isaac returned to Grantham and a year later he began studying at Trinity College, Cambridge.

When Hannah married the Reverend Smith, she had made sure that he provided a sum of money for Isaac. But there was not enough to pay for his university studies and food, so he had to enrol as a "subsizar." This meant that he had to pay his way by doing certain chores, such as waiting on his tutor at the dining table.

From an early age, Isaac seems to have kept almost everything he wrote, including all his detailed notebooks. By reading these, historians have discovered exactly what he was taught at Cambridge, and how his ideas changed as he grew older. The

science that university students learned in the seventeenth century was based on knowledge that had been handed down from hundreds of years earlier. It included the teachings of the famous Greek thinker Aristotle, who lived two thousand years before Isaac Newton. In his notebooks, Newton wrote about the ideas of Aristotle, and also about the theories of new thinkers, such as the Italian Galileo Galilei and the Frenchman René Descartes. These men argued against the beliefs of Aristotle and said that science should be looked at in a different way. Newton had to study the ancient teachings because he would have to take examinations on them, but he believed that the new thinkers were right. Although he did not agree with everything they said, he knew that the study of science had to change.

In 1665 the Bubonic Plague was raging. In London alone more than 7,000 people were dying every week and the disease was spreading through the eastern counties of England. It reached Cambridge in the autumn. The university colleges were ordered to shut down and the students left to seek safety elsewhere. Newton, who had graduated earlier in the year, was among them. He went back to Woolsthorpe to wait for the plague to pass. Apart from one or two brief visits to Cambridge, he stayed in the country for the next eighteen months. During that time he made some of the greatest discoveries in the history of science. To realize just how important Newton's work was, we must first look at the scientific teachings that were accepted at the time, and at the new science that was emerging.

The plague frequently swept through Europe in the seventeenth century. It reached London in 1603, 1625 and again in 1665, when 80,000 people are thought to have died.

2 ▼ Aristotle and the New Science

Most seventeenth-century science was based on the work of the Ancient Greek thinker Aristotle, who lived from 384 to 322 BC. But why was this? When the Crusaders of the eleventh, twelfth and thirteenth centuries recaptured parts of the Holy Land from the Arabs, Christian scholars brought back to Europe huge quantities of manuscripts. Among them were Arabic versions of the writings of the Ancient Greek philosophers. One of them, Aristotle, came to be regarded as the source of all knowledge. He had brought together all the teachings of his own civilization and that of earlier ones. He had written on a huge range of subjects, including what we today call physics, chemistry, biology, astronomy, cosmology, geology, politics, poetry and much more. Some of his teachings went against the beliefs of the all-powerful Catholic Church. But gradually they were altered slightly so that there was no conflict with the Church.

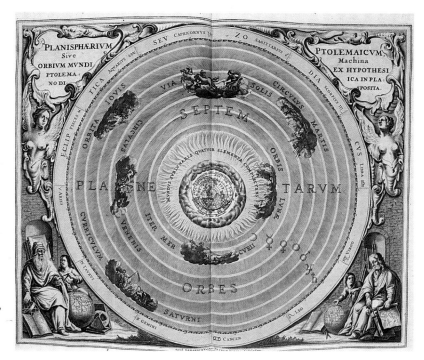

An illustration showing the four elements that, according to the Ancient Greek philosophers, made up the Universe. The Earth is surrounded by the other three elements – water, air and fire.

Eventually, to argue against Aristotle was to doubt God's view of the world as portrayed in the Bible.

One of the reasons for this was that Aristotle's ideas appeared to make a great deal of common sense. He believed that everything in the world had its own natural form or appearance, and its true purpose was to reach that form. For example, the purpose of a seed was to develop into a fully-grown plant, that of a baby was to grow to become an adult. The whole of nature was governed by order and purpose.

Most people in the ancient world believed that all the planets orbited around the Earth and that the Sun was merely one of the planets. In the third century BC, the Greek Aristarchus argued that the Sun, not the Earth, was at the center of the Universe. But Aristotle said this could not be true. After all, the Sun rises every day in the east and sets in the west. Furthermore, if the Earth were moving around the Sun, anything that was not attached to its surface would fly off into space.

Aristotle identified two types of motion on Earth, the "natural" motions of things trying to reach their natural places, and the "forced" motions of objects that are moved by a living thing, such as a stone thrown by a person. Both types of motion have a beginning and an end, but what about the motions of the planets, spinning around the Earth without ever stopping? To explain these, Aristotle imagined a fifth, perfect, element called "ether." He argued that everything in the Universe that was farther away from the Earth than the Moon was made of ether which, because it was perfect, never changed. So the planets moved endlessly around the Earth in perfect, circular orbits.

During the fourteenth and fifteenth centuries, people began to question Aristotle's ideas. By the sixteenth century much of his teaching was openly disputed. The problem was to find something to take its place.

Nicolaus Copernicus (1473–1543) proposed that the Sun was at the center of the Universe and the planets revolved around it in circular orbits. But he could not

Aristotle's Universe

The Greeks believed that everything on Earth was made of a mixture of four pure elements, *earth, air, fire* and *water*. Aristotle developed this idea further. He noticed that each of the four elements seemed to move in a particular direction. The heavier elements – water and earthy matter – fell downward, while the lighter ones – air and fire – moved upward. Thinking back to his idea that all living things tried to grow into their natural form, he decided that each of the elements must have a similar purpose – to find its natural place in the Universe. He thought that the Universe was trying to achieve its "natural" arrangement – an earthy body at the center surrounded by layers of water, air and fire – and that the only thing that prevented this perfect arrangement was the movement of the Sun, which "stirred up" the elements. Nonetheless, to Aristotle, the Earth itself was clearly in its natural place, and there was no reason why it should move, either around the Sun or anywhere else. This illustration from Aristotle's *Meteorologia* shows the comets and meteors, which were his "fiery elements."

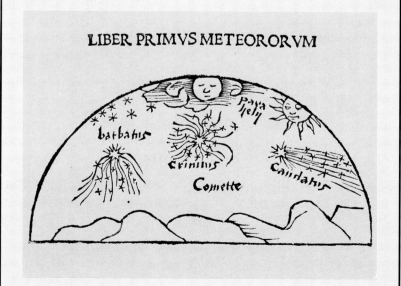

The Copernican system of the Universe placed the Sun at the center with the planets orbiting around it. The figure at the bottom right is Copernicus himself.

explain why things did not fly off into space as the Earth revolved around the Sun. Other people turned to the magical beliefs of the ancient world in the hope of finding the key to the Universe.

While he was at Cambridge, Newton studied the teachings of Aristotle. But he was far more interested in the ideas of the "new scientists" such as Galileo (1564–1642) and Descartes (1596–1650). They seriously questioned the science of Aristotle without relying on magic. They believed a theory had to be tested before it could be accepted as true. It was not enough simply to observe what happened and try to think about why it happened. Careful experiments had to be carried out to explain how it happened.

Galileo's telescope revealed new worlds previously unseen by humans, including the four moons of the planet Jupiter.

Galileo was one of the first scientists to put these beliefs into practice. In 1609, while he was Professor of Mathematics in Padua, Italy, he heard about a fascinating new invention – the telescope. Galileo set about discovering how it worked and quickly built himself a much better version. He realized that his telescope was not just a practical tool, useful for spotting ships out at sea; it could also be used for research. Turning it toward the night sky, he saw some startling things. He found that the Moon was not the perfect body described by Aristotle, but had craters and mountains on its surface. He also discovered that the Earth was not the only planet to have a moon – Jupiter had no less than four. These and other discoveries convinced him that Copernicus was right: the Sun, not the Earth, was at the center of the Universe. This put Galileo in direct conflict with the Catholic Church, which still insisted that the Earth was stationary at the center of the Universe.

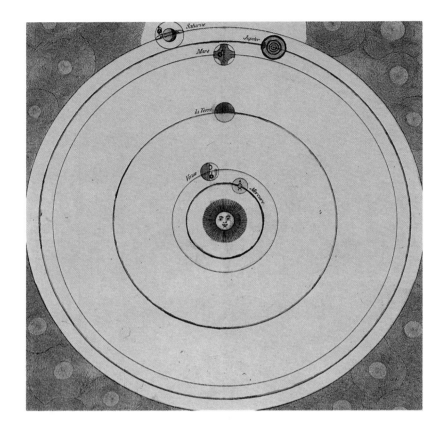

Descartes had a great influence on scientific thinking in the seventeenth century. His system of the Universe, with its "vortices" whirling in space, is shown here.

Descartes had a rather different idea of the Universe and its workings. He believed that it was a kind of giant machine that had been made by God. The Universe was filled with "ether," a transparent fluid that swirled around in huge whirlpools called "vortices." At the center of one of these vortices was the Sun, with the planets moving around it. Descartes believed that the movements of the vortices explained the motions of the Earth and the planets, gravity, magnetism and even the beating of the human heart.

Yet for all his talk about the need to test scientific theories by observation and experiment, Descartes did not check his own theories in this way. Although he

14

René Descartes (1596–1650).

knew that mathematics was the key to scientific knowledge, he did not work out his own ideas mathematically. Nonetheless his work inspired many other scientists. At about this time they began to form the first scientific societies, with the intention of collecting and exchanging ideas in the search for truth. In 1662 the Royal Society of London was founded, followed four years later by the French Royal Academy of Sciences. Besides wanting to share and to communicate scientific information, these societies – and others that followed them later – committed themselves to the investigation of nature through experiment. The "new science" was becoming accepted as the true way to promote learning and understanding in science.

3 Light and Color

Back at Woolsthorpe, waiting for the plague to leave Cambridge, Newton thought about the ideas of the new scientists and of Descartes, in particular. They excited him, even though he knew that Descartes had not obeyed his own rules about checking his theories. He also thought about mathematics, and that was the field in which he was to make some of his greatest discoveries.

Among the first of his successes was the invention of what he called "fluxions." This very powerful mathematical technique (now known as calculus) is still used today. Newton did not tell anyone of his discovery. Instead he used fluxions to make his other discoveries and then wrote them out in conventional mathematics.

Early in 1666 Newton began experimenting with light, lenses and prisms. Like Descartes before him, he was trying to find a way of making a better telescope. Even in Aristotle's day people had known that if sunlight passed through a glass prism the light that emerged from the other side was colored.

The accepted reason for this was that the prism "stained" or darkened the sunlight. Light passing through the thinnest part of the prism was darkened a little to become red. At the thickest part of the prism it was darkened much more to become violet, and in between were the other colors of the rainbow. To most people this was common sense, but Newton realized it did not explain why light enters the prism as a disk – the shape of the Sun – but comes out again in long, narrow strips.

He carried out a series of experiments to find out why this happens. He made the beam of sunlight pass through different parts of the prism to show that the

Colors of Light

Newton set up this experiment for himself. He adjusted the shutters on his window so that sunlight shone through a prism and onto a wall. As he expected, the light that came out of the prism was in the colors of the rainbow – violet, indigo, blue, green, yellow, orange and red.

thickness of the glass did not cause this effect. Then he made sure that the shape of the colored spectrum was not the result of a faulty prism. He wondered if the light that emerged from the prism moved in a curve rather than a straight line, but he soon proved otherwise. Newton's next experiment was critical. He allowed light to pass through the prism and emerge in colored bands. Then he selected one of the colored bands and placed another prism in its path. Instead of being darkened even more by the second prism, the light stayed exactly the same color. He repeated this for each color in turn with the same result. This proved that white light – natural sunlight – was a mixture of light of different colors. It was not darkened as it passed through a prism, but was actually separated into these different colors. Once it had been separated it could not be split up any further. The colors appeared to fan out in a series of bands because the prism slightly altered the direction in which the light traveled as it passed through. Violet light was bent, or refracted, more than indigo, which was refracted more than blue, and so on. As Newton wrote: ". . . *Light* consists of *Rays differently refrangible* which . . . were . . . according to their degrees of refrangibility, transmitted towards divers parts of the wall. What is more," he continued, "I have often with Admiration beheld that all the Colours of the Prisme being made to converge, and thereby to be again mixed, reproduced light, intirely and perfectly white."

Newton had returned to Trinity College, Cambridge, in 1667. He continued to experiment with light but did not publish his discovery. However, he seems to have told Isaac Barrow, the Professor of Mathematics, because shortly afterward Barrow wrote that Newton was a "man of quite exceptional ability." In 1669, when Barrow resigned as Professor, the person chosen to succeed him was Isaac Newton. He was 26 years old.

Newton now abandoned his attempts to perfect the telescope by grinding specially shaped lenses. He had

Right Some illustrations from the pages of Newton's Opticks in which he shows how a rainbow is formed (figures 14 and 15) and how light is split by a prism.

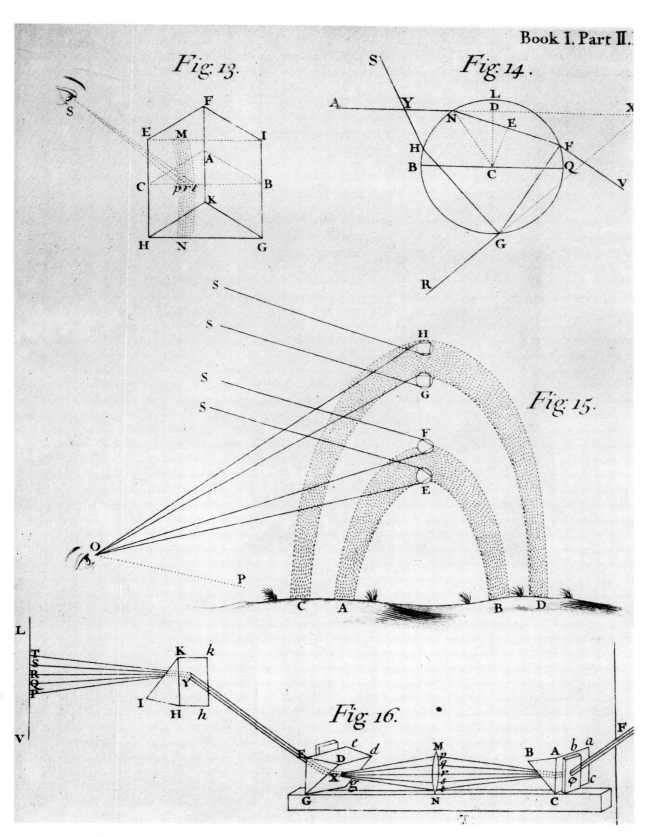

Fig: 13.

Fig: 14.

Fig: 15.

Fig: 16.

19

been trying to make lenses that were non-spherical. This was because when normal, spherical lenses were used, fuzzy fringes appeared around the edges. His experiments with light and color led him to believe that this problem could not be overcome. (He was, in fact, wrong about this but it was almost a hundred years before his mistake was discovered.)

Newton's reflecting telescope.

Newton's Telescope

The first telescope was invented in 1608 by a Dutch instrument maker, Hans Lippershey. His type of telescope – called a refracting telescope – uses a lens to collect light rays and bring them together at the eyepiece, where they are magnified. Newton designed a new type of telescope, which used mirrors to collect the light and then redirect it to the eyepiece at the side of the tube. Newton's telescope is called a reflecting telescope. Many of the huge modern telescopes used in observatories are of this type.

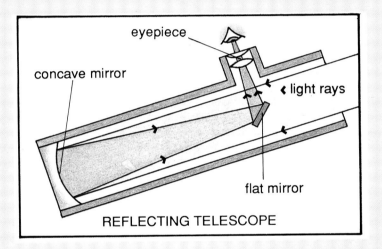

REFLECTING TELESCOPE

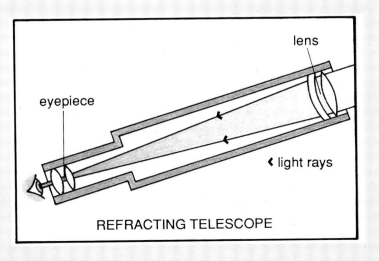

REFRACTING TELESCOPE

In the meantime he developed a completely new type of telescope, which used a mirror rather than a lens to focus light onto the eyepiece. News of his reflecting telescope reached the newly formed Royal Society in London, and in 1671 he sent them one as a gift. It caused something of a stir, and the following year Newton was elected a Fellow of the Society. A week after his election he wrote to Henry Oldenburg, the Secretary, saying that he would like to tell the Society about the important discovery that had led him to build his telescope.

Newton's own drawing of his reflecting telescope. Notice the eyepiece. Observers no longer had to adopt an uncomfortable position to view the stars with this type of telescope.

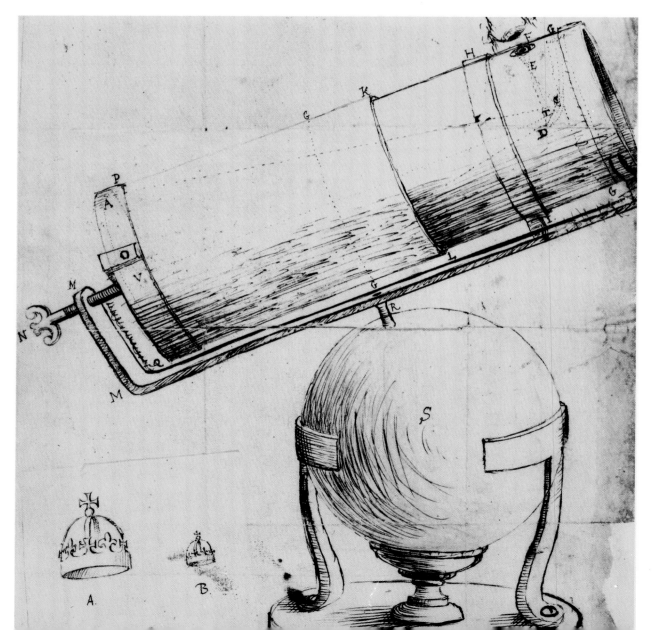

Newton's Rings

Among the discoveries Newton described in *Opticks* were what we now call Newton's Rings. He noticed that when a curved lens is placed on top of a flat sheet of glass and light is shone down through the lens, a series of colored rings appears. The rings are caused by the fact that some light is reflected from the bottom of the lens and some from the top of the glass sheet, which is a very small distance below the lens. Sometimes these two reflected light rays produce a dark ring. Next to each dark ring is a bright one, resulting from the combined strength of the light rays. These Newton's rings (below) are obtained by placing glass microscope slides in contact with each other.

This illustration of Newton's colored rings is from a popular book explaining Newton's ideas, Mathematical Elements of Natural Philosophy Confirm'd by Experiments, *published in 1747.*

A few weeks later Newton sent the Society a short paper describing his experiments and putting forward his conclusion that white light was actually a mixture of colors. This idea was totally against the teachings of the Ancients and even the theories of Descartes. None of his contemporaries would accept it, and Newton found himself drawn into in a series of bitter arguments, especially with Robert Hooke. Hooke believed that light was made up of a number of vibrations, each of which produced a different color when it passed through a prism. Newton replied that his experiments had proved this was not the case, but the arguments continued.

In the end Newton became disillusioned. He was proud of his discovery and felt that he had given something important to the world, only to have it thrown back at him. He wrote to Gottfried Wilhelm von Leibniz, a fellow mathematician: "I was so persecuted with discussions arising from the publication of my theory of light that I blamed my own imprudence for parting with so substantial a blessing as my quiet to run after a shadow." From then on Newton refused to enter into debates about his work, particularly with Robert Hooke. He carried on his experiments with optics and made further discoveries. But he kept them to himself until he published his book *Opticks* in 1704, the year after Hooke died.

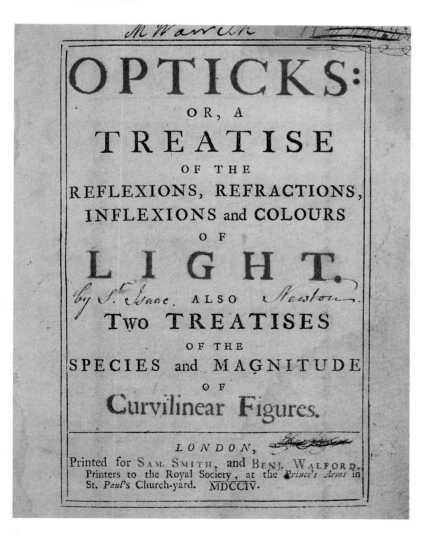

The title page of Newton's Opticks, *published in 1704. This work was more easily understood by ordinary people than the earlier* Principia.

4

Gravity, Astronomy and Motion

Of all his achievements, Newton is best known for his discovery of the laws of movement and gravitation. Like his study of light and refraction, this work had its beginnings in the "plague years" at Woolsthorpe. The

There is a popular story that Newton's theory of gravity came to him when he was sitting in the orchard at Woolsthorpe. Newton himself is said to have told it to his friends.

Johannes Kepler based his laws of planetary movement entirely on observation. Newton was able to prove them correct mathematically, using calculus and his new ideas of gravity and the laws of motion.

story goes that one day, while he was sitting in his mother's orchard, Newton noticed an apple fall from a tree to the ground. This started him thinking about one of the most important scientific questions of his time. It was to do with the planets and how they move around the Sun.

Aristotle had stated that the Moon, the Sun and all the planets move around the Earth inside a series of hollow spheres. Copernicus also believed that the planets revolved in circular orbits, but around the Sun, not the Earth. Gradually the idea of hollow spheres came to be challenged. In the early seventeenth century another astronomer, Johannes Kepler, thought that there might be a force radiating outward from the Sun, holding each planet in its correct orbit. No one paid much attention to his theory, but in trying to prove it he made another startling discovery. He found that the orbits of the planets were not circular at all, but elliptical, like flattened circles. Kepler also worked out a relationship between the time a planet takes to orbit the Sun and its average distance from the Sun.

The movement of the planets and an explanation of Kepler's theories was interesting other leading scientists as well as Newton. A Dutch astronomer, Christiaan Huygens, began to investigate the forces at work when objects moved in circles. His work was taken up by three prominent English scientists, Edmund Halley, Robert Hooke and Christopher Wren,

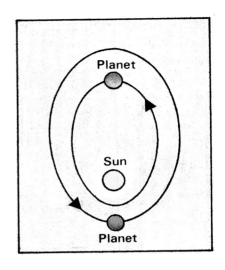

Kepler observed that the path of the planets around the Sun was elliptical, not circular. He also found a relationship between the time it took a planet to orbit the Sun and its distance from it. A planet twice as far away from the Sun will take four times as long to orbit it.

Left *Christiaan Huygens (1629–95) is credited with the design of the first practical pendulum clock.*

Sir Christopher Wren (1632–1723) was one of the founding members of the Royal Society in 1662. He was an astronomer, but is better known as the architect who designed St. Paul's Cathedral and more than fifty other London churches after the Great Fire of London 1666.

members of the Royal Society. They too examined the motions of bodies moving in circular orbits. Their investigations suggested that the orbits of the planets around the Sun would be circular if there was a special "inverse square" relationship between them. This means to say that if one planet is twice the distance of another from the Sun, the force of attraction to the Sun will be a quarter of that felt by the nearer planet. If a planet is three times as far away, then the attraction will be only one ninth, and so on. Although they agreed on the inverse square relationship, none of the three was able to explain why the orbits of the planets were elliptical.

Hoping to find help, in 1684 Halley visited Newton in Cambridge. He was surprised to find that Newton had also discovered the inverse square relationship between the Sun and the planets, and had worked out mathematically that the orbits resulting from this relationship would be an ellipse. Newton was unable to find the proof among his papers and so he promised to write it out again and send it to Halley.

It was another two years before Newton completed his work in full and presented it in the form of a manuscript to the Royal Society. During that time Halley encouraged him constantly and eventually paid for the book to be published because the Society was short of funds. Finally, in May 1687, the *Mathematical Principles of Natural Philosophy*, or *Principia*, as it has become known, appeared. From the moment it was published it caused a sensation – Newton's mathematical proof had expanded into a volume that

Edmund Halley (1656–1742) was an astronomer and mathematician. His greatest contribution to science was in the study of comets. In 1680 he observed a comet that appeared over Paris, worked out its orbit, and predicted its return in 1758. It is now known as Halley's Comet.

An example of Newton's First Law of Motion: container ships like this have so much inertia that they have to begin slowing down over a mile from where they are to dock.

showed how a single law could be used to explain the movements of the Sun and the planets and the motion of objects on the Earth. Even the ebb and flow of the tides could be explained by this law.

Newton's first achievement in the *Principia* was to define how forces, including gravity, acted. He summarized this in three basic laws, now known as Newton's Laws of Motion.

The First Law states that a body will stay at rest (if it is not already moving) or will continue to move at the same speed and in a straight line (if it is already moving) unless an outside force acts upon it. This tendency of all bodies to carry on with whatever motion they have is called inertia.

Newton's Second Law states that a moving body moves faster, or accelerates, when a force acts on it. It accelerates in the direction of the force, and the amount of acceleration depends on the size of the force and the mass of the object. (So, an empty shopping cart will be easier to push than a full one; a light stone will be easier to throw than a heavy one.)

Right Newton's Third Law of Motion. Sprinters using starting blocks to push themselves forward at the start of a race.

Left In the 1980s javelin throwers were throwing so far that they began to endanger crowds in the stadium. The International Amateur Athletics Federation made the javelin heavier, and the distances thrown became less, illustrating Newton's Second

Newton's Third Law says that forces always act in pairs. If you push or pull an object, it will push or pull you in return and with equal force. So, for example, if you stand on a skateboard and push backward against the ground with one foot you will begin to move forward. The ground has pushed you in the opposite direction to your own push. These two forces are known as "action" and "reaction." Newton summarized this in his Third Law of Motion: "The force that body A exerts on body B is always equal and opposite to the force that body B exerts on body A."

Newton dealt with the laws governing forces and the movement of objects on the Earth in the first part of the *Principia*. He went on to develop his ideas about gravitation and the workings of the Universe. He argued that just as gravitation attracts an apple to the Earth's surface so it pulls the Moon toward the Earth and keeps it in orbit. Moreover, Newton realized that the same force of attraction exists between all bodies in the Universe. Gravitation was the single force holding the entire Universe together.

Right *A satellite orbiting the Earth. The pull of the Earth's gravity keeps satellites in orbit and prevents them from moving off into space.*

Left *The launch of an American Saturn 1B rocket. The thrust from the rocket's engines is directed downward and, as Newton's Third Law predicts, this produces an equal and opposite force, pushing the rocket upward.*

In the pages of the *Principia*, then, Newton used his laws of motion and the effects of forces to solve many of the problems that had been debated by scientists for centuries. This one book marked the start of the development of modern science. For more than two hundred years it was almost a bible for astronomers and other scientists. Even today the Laws of Motion are the basis of all mechanical science.

5

Middle and Later Life

Following the writing and publication of the *Principia* Newton returned to his duties as Professor of Mathematics at Trinity College, Cambridge. In 1685 King Charles II died and James II succeeded him. The new monarch was a Roman Catholic, and his religious beliefs were to interrupt the workings of Cambridge University and of Newton himself.

Early in 1687, James II attempted to force the University of Cambridge to give a degree to a Benedictine monk, Father Alban Francis. When the University refused, the Vice-Chancellor and other senior officials, including Newton, were summoned to

appear before the notoriously severe judge, George Jeffreys. Although he was not a Catholic himself, Jeffreys was willing to support James II in his efforts to make Britain adopt Catholicism as its official religion. Jeffreys would not listen to the arguments of the University officials and he stripped the Vice-Chancellor, John Peachell, of his position.

The following year James II was forced into exile when the Protestant William of Orange replaced him as king. Peachell was restored as Vice-Chancellor. Newton had played an important part in the University's attempts to obstruct James II, and in 1689 he was rewarded by being elected Member of Parliament for Cambridge. He does not seem to have played an important part in the proceedings of Parliament. It is thought that he spoke only once and that was to ask someone to open a window. Parliament was dissolved in 1690 and Newton went back to Cambridge to continue his mathematical work. This work was to be interrupted yet again, but this time it was by illness.

During the previous few years Newton had worked extremely hard. The writing of *Principia* had demanded tremendous concentration and he had rarely gone to bed before two o'clock in the morning, and frequently it had been as late as five or six. After about four hours' sleep he would get up and start working again. This and other stresses upon him took their toll, and in 1693 he had a nervous breakdown. He recovered quickly, and by 1694 he was hard at work again. In 1695 Newton became Warden of the Mint in London.

While he was Warden, Newton was able to continue his duties at Cambridge. But in 1699 he was made Master of the Mint and he soon had to appoint a deputy to take care of some of his university work. In 1701 he was re-elected as Member of Parliament for Cambridge. Then, in 1703, he was made President of the Royal Society. This was a great honor, and he was to be re-elected every year for the rest of his life.

Left Newton's dog knocked over a candle and set fire to his papers. He lost twenty years' work in the fire and had to start again from scratch.

Above The Royal Mint, London, as it was at the beginning of the nineteenth century.

Left Isaac Newton's house in London as it was in about 1850.

A few years earlier Newton had begun to quarrel with some of his fellow scientists. While he was working at the Mint, he was annoyed when the Astronomer Royal, John Flamsteed, spread a rumor that Newton was about to publish an improved version of his theory about the motion of the Moon. Newton responded by saying he had no wish to be "teased by foreigners about mathematical things or to be thought . . . to be trifling away my time about them, when I should be about the King's business." Following this and other

Newton at the Royal Mint

In 1695 Newton left Cambridge and moved to London. Charles Montague, a former student who had gone into politics, was now Chancellor of the Exchequer. He arranged for Newton to be appointed to the post of Warden of the Royal Mint. Montague had decided to call in all of the coins that were in use in Britain. He intended to melt them down and reissue them in a new design. The reason was that pieces of the old gold and silver coins were frequently cut off around the edges. This meant that the value of the currency was being reduced. The edges of the new coins were to be marked, or "milled," so that it would be obvious if they had been "clipped." Montague knew that this huge task would be impossible unless it was properly organized, and he wanted Newton to take charge of it. In fact, the whole operation took only two years to complete. This medal showing Newton's portrait was struck in 1726.

disagreements, Newton made sure that the control of the publication of his life's work in astronomy was taken out of Flamsteed's hands. Newton also began a bitter argument with the German scientist Gottfried Wilhelm von Leibniz who, like Newton, claimed to have discovered calculus. We now know that Leibniz did, quite independently, discover it at the same time as Newton. But when the Royal Society set up a committee to look into the affair, Newton made it appear that Leibniz had stolen his idea.

The controversy with Leibniz about calculus blew up around the same time as the publication of *Opticks* in 1704. It proved to be a very popular book and Newton himself worked on the second and third editions that were published during his lifetime. Also at about the same time, Queen Anne visited Cambridge and knighted Newton.

In 1725 Newton moved out of London to this house in what was then the village of Kensington.

Throughout his later life Newton continued in his role as President of the Royal Society. From about 1722 he began to suffer ill health, and in 1725 he moved out of the middle of London to what was then the village of Kensington, where the air was healthier. Not long after moving he became seriously ill. On the morning of March 20, 1727 he died, and eight days later, he was buried in Westminster Abbey, London.

During his eighty-five-year life, Newton effectively invented modern science. He constructed his scientific theories after a great deal of observation and experiment, and then tested most of them and cross-checked them until he was sure they were correct. These methods were quite new in his day, and the determination with which he tested his ideas was previously unheard-of.

Newton became a famous figure. This print was sold with the verse, "See the great Newton, He who first survey'd The plan by which the Universe was made..."

Many modern observatories rely on Newtonian reflecting telescopes.

His invention of calculus would have been enough to guarantee him a place in history, but that was only the beginning. One of the marks of his genius was that he asked simple questions that everyone else thought had obvious answers. His experiments with light and prisms overturned the ideas that had been held for centuries and became the basis for the scientific study of color. The reflecting telescope, invented by Newton as a result of his light experiments, is still in use today. Its full potential was realized only when it became possible to make accurate parabolic mirrors, and some of the world's most famous astronomical observatories rely on powerful reflecting telescopes.

This picture shows Newton's apple tree in 1840.

Newton also developed a theory about the way in which light was transmitted. His idea, that light was a mixture of tiny particles called corpuscles that produced waves as they traveled, caused a great deal of controversy. It fell from favor during the nineteenth century when most scientists thought that light was made up purely of waves. But since 1905, when Albert Einstein wrote about particles of light called photons, many people have pointed out the similarity of that idea to Newton's.

His crowning glory was the *Principia*. For more than two hundred years this work stood as the accepted mathematical law that explained the workings of the entire Universe. Not until the early years of this century was Newton's idea of universal gravitation superseded. Again it was Einstein, with his theory of relativity, who was to turn science upside down.

Yet, for all of his scientific brilliance, there was another side to Newton that he kept secret. For much of his life he practiced alchemy. He was also deeply interested in and influenced by religion. He believed that everything written in the Bible was literally true and wrote huge books in which he tried to prove that the Revelation of St. John, the last book in the Bible, had accurately predicted the course of ancient history. He was convinced that the inverse square law had been discovered hundreds of years earlier by the Greek mathematician Pythagoras. He clung to these beliefs even while his own scientific work was destroying their foundations. However, none of this can belittle Newton's achievements; he was without doubt one of the greatest scientists the world has ever seen.

Newton's theories were quickly accepted during and after his lifetime. This illustration explaining the Third Law of Motion comes from a physics book published in 1747.

Left *Newton's memorial statue at Trinity College, Cambridge.*

Date Chart

1642   Isaac Newton born at Woolsthorpe, Lincolnshire, in England.

1645   Left in the care of his grandmother when his mother remarried.

1655–58   Studied at King's School, Grantham.

1661   Entered Trinity College, Cambridge.

1665   Graduated from university; returned to Woolsthorpe because of the plague. Developed ideas on calculus, optics and gravitation.

1667   Returned to Cambridge.

1669   Elected Professor of Mathematics.

1671   Sent his reflecting telescope to Royal Society.

1672   Submitted his theory of light and color to Royal Society; elected Fellow of Royal Society.

1684   Halley visited Cambridge and Newton began writing the *Principia*.

1687   Publication of the *Principia*.

1689   Elected Member of Parliament for Cambridge.

1693   Nervous breakdown.

1695   Moved from Cambridge to London; appointed Warden of Royal Mint.

1996–99   Revised coinage of the realm.

1699   Appointed Master of the Mint.

1701   Re-elected Member of Parliament, and resigned from duties at Cambridge.

1703   Elected President of Royal Society.

1704   Publication of *Opticks*.

1705   Knighted by Queen Anne. Controversy with Leibniz over the development of calculus.

1725   Moved to Kensington.

1727   Died; buried in Westminster Abbey.

Picture acknowledgments

Allsport 33; Ann Ronan Picture Library iii, 4, 9, 11, 12, 14, 15, 17, 19, 24, 25, 28, 36, 38, 45; Bruce Coleman 34, 35; Camera Press 32; Michael Holford 20, 39, 40; National Portrait Gallery cover; Royal Society 5, 7, 22, 41, 42, 44, 45; Science Museum 27, 30; J-L Charmet/Science Photo Library 26; David Parker/Science Photo Library 23; Topham 31; Wayland Picture Library 13, 28; Zefa 43. Illustrations Solum A. Wan cover; Peter Smith 21, 28.

Glossary

Alchemy   The "science" of trying to turn base metals, such as lead, into pure gold or into substances that would give eternal life.

Astronomy   The scientific study of the Sun, planets and the rest of space.

Body   (in physics) Any physical object.

Calculus   A special technique invented by Newton and, at the same time, by Leibniz, used to solve many mathematical problems.

Cosmology   The science of the Universe.

Ellipse   An oval shape.

Elliptical   Shaped like an ellipse.

Ether   To Aristotle, the fifth natural element, thought to be purer than the other four: earth, water, air and fire.

Force   The push or pull that makes something move, slows it down or stops it.

Gravitation   The force of attraction between any two objects in the Universe.

Gravity   Force that attracts objects toward the center of the Earth or other planets.

Inertia   The natural force in matter that makes a body remain at rest or keep on moving in the same direction and in a straight line, unless it is acted upon by an outside force.

Mass   The amount of matter contained in a body.

Matter   The material that makes up a physical object.

Optics   The science relating to sight and the laws of light.

Parabola   A special type of curve. Parabolic mirrors are used in some kinds of telescopes to collect light.

Prism   A glass block, usually with triangular ends, which can be used to break up white light into the colors of the rainbow.

Refraction   The breaking or bending of rays of light. For example, light is refracted where it enters water at a slant.

Refrangible   Able to be refracted.

Spectrum   The band of colors into which a beam of light can be separated or broken down.

Weight   The measure of the force of gravity, which is pulling a body to the Earth.

Books to Read

Force: The Power Behind Movement by Eric Laithwaite (Franklin Watts, 1986)

Halley's Comet: What We've Learned by Gregory Vogt (Watts, 1987)

... ∩da Walpole (Warwick, 1987)

...rs by Kathryn Whyman

Physics: From Newton to the Big Bang by Albert & Eve Stwertka (Watts, 1986)

Rainbows to Lasers: Projects with Light by Kathryn Whyman (Gloucester, 1989)

The Solar System by David Lambert (Bookwright, 1984)

The Space Telescope by Christopher Lampton (Watts, 1987)

Index

48

398609

jB McTavish, Douglas
NEWTON
Isaac Newton

$12.40

DATE			